Updated Knowledge Lighthouse

A SKILL-BASED COURSE ON GENERAL KNOWLEDGE

3

Name : ....

Grade: .... Section : ....

Different animals eat different foods. Match the animal to the food they eat.

Seema Chari • Kunal Savarkar

HarperCollins*Publishers*

Publishing operations in 17 countries and 120+ imprints globally

William Collins' dream of knowledge for all began with the publication of his first book in 1819. A self-educated mill worker, he not only enriched millions of lives, but also founded a flourishing publishing house. Today, staying true to this spirit, Collins books are packed with inspiration, innovation and practical expertise. They place you at the centre of a world of possibility and give you exactly what you need to explore it.

Published by Collins Learning
An imprint of HarperCollins*Publishers* India
Building No. 10, Tower A, 4th Floor, DLF Cyber City, Gurugram, Haryana 122002, India

First edition: 2025
Reprint: 10 9 8 7 6 5 4 3 2 1
ISBN: 978-93-6213-819-4

Artwork, typesetting and layout by **Toon Fantasy and Majik Strokes, GNZE Interactions**
Printed and bound in India by Saurabh Printers Pvt.Ltd.

ACKNOWLEDGEMENTS

Cover and title page images: Anastasiia Ovsiannykova

Inside: Title page: Violetta Myroshnichenk; **Icons:** Hiranmay Baidya, LvNL, cienpies, KaanC; impulse50; **4:** Natalia Darmoroz, impulse50, ONYXprj; **5:** Natalia Darmoroz, ONYXprj, Magnilion, colematt; **6:** Natalia Darmoroz, impulse50, ONYXprj; **8:** Natalia Darmoroz, impulse50, ONYXprj; **9:** Gabi Wolf; **11:** eliflamra; **12:** colematt; **13:** svaga; **14:** colematt, svaga; **15:** svaga, Rohit Kumar; **16:** red_frog, Tribalium, AzFree, Thomas Lydell, Sylfide, Makoto Hara, Taras Dubov; **17:** AlexStar, mayakova, Anastasiia_New, DoggieMonkey, Suraj Raheja, Mark Astakhov, Leya1703, Rohit Kumar; **19:** colematt, Mimosa Studio; lucentius, Berezka_Klo, Nora Carol Photography, Turqay Melikli, abstractdesignlabs, Thomas Lydell, kolotuschenko, THEPALMER, cnythzl, kathykonkle, KristinaVelickovic, matteodestefano, ilyaliren, Easy_Company, SENRYU, Judy Unger, cako74, bortonia, Yuliia Sydorova; **20:** ivanastar, Empato, JacquesPALUT, S_A_N, martince2, TanawatPontchour, Aleksandra Nigmatulina, goodmoments, Muhammad Ahmad Jumasa; **21:** Tim Whitby, Craig Barritt, LMPC; Orthosie; Ls9907; The India Today Group; **27:** Baron; **28:** svaga; **29:** svaga, robuart, GlinskajaOlga; **30:** FreezingRain, fortise, South_agency, Liudmila Chernetska; **31:** kiankhoon, skynesher, hxdyl, warrengoldswain, svetikd, puhhha, Elena Istomina; **32:** colematt, panimoni; **33:** Trifonenko, colematt, zaricm, panimoni; **36:** Tarzan9280, Skouatroulio, stereostok, Ivanvieito, maodesign, Ludovic Debono; **37:** Amorphis, m_pavlov; **40:** GlobalP, Coldimages, CoreyFord, spxChrome, thawats, GlobalP, omega77, nattanan726, Ztranger, GlobalP; **41:** Henrik_L, BZH22, abadonian, Ale-ks, xjbxjhxm, MirekKijewski, t_lesiv, smuay, CreativeNature_nl, abadonian, 3drenderings, CoreyFord; **42:** Stringer, Indranil Mukherjee, Paul Kane, Michael Dodge, Ankur Salvi-IDI, Tim Clayton - Corbis, Albert Perez, Atsushi Tomura, Cameron Spencer, Anadolu Agency; **43:** Dave Thompson, David Cannon, Arun Sankar, Pacific Press, Sajjad Hussain, David Cannon; **44:** PeterPencil; **45:** liangpv, RM80, PeterPencil; **46:** olegtoka, colematt, trismile, eduardrobert, Daria_Andrianova, ChubarovY, RedVector, Nadzeya_Dzivakova, doomu, jehsomwang, Pavel Naumov, Hanna Ferentc; **47:** macy75, MariaTkach, blueringmedia, Evgenii_Bobrov, Lcosmo, studiogstock, vectortatu, RamCreativ, bombuscreative, archivector, Olesya Chesnokova; **48:** © Jennifer Borton; **52:** janrysavy; **53:** Ian McKinnell; **54:** Topical Press Agency, William Vandivert, Science & Society Picture Library, Mondadori Portfolio, Michael Nicholson, DEA / Biblioteca Ambrosiana; **56:** milbarb, blueringmedia, blueringmedia, Muhammad Zakky Fathony, eliflamra, eliflamra; **58:** Narinder Nanu, ChandraDhas, Hindustan Times, Hindustan Times; **59:** colematt, klyaksun; **60:** Poligrafistka; **63:** holgs, saiko3p, Rudr Peter, saiko3p, Purplexsu, saiko3p; **65:** Angelika, andDraw, Derek Brumby, Franck Fife, Matt Roberts, FRANCK FIFE/Contributor, khvost; **67:** tnotn, Creativeye99, Model-la, tobiasjo, upthebanner, andriano_cz, Keith Lance, Art Wager; **69:** WesAbrams; **70:** Majority World, JosuOzkaritz, Balaji Srinivasan; **71:** befehr, kathykonkle, Magnilion, MichikoDesign; **72:** IndiaPictures, Danielrao, davidevison, KR photography; **73:** saiko3p, NurPhoto, ePhotocorp, Andrii Fomenko; **74:** G0d4ather, Poligrafistka, dikobraziy, Bigpra; **75:** Alisovna; **76:** CSA Images; **77:** ileezhun, InfiniteGraphic, Fidan Babayeva, © Jennifer Borton, Serhii Brovko; **78:** Bettmann, mantosh; **79:** Poligrafistka

SDG logo and icons: https://www.un.org/sustainabledevelopment/

The content of this publication has not been approved by the United Nations and does not reflect the views of the United Nations or its officials or Member States.

Browse the complete Collins catalogue at www.collins.in.
For any queries/feedback, please write to us at SCHOOLSUPPORT@harpercollins.co.in.

Preface

Like the universe, knowledge, too, is limitless. No matter how much we know, there is always more to know. In the 21st century, thanks to the leaps that technology has made and continues to make, we shall have to gather knowledge throughout our lives; so much so that we have coined a new portmanteau, to describe it: 'upskilling'.

Another novelty of the third millennium is how we access and absorb knowledge. Apart from human sources (family, teachers, friends), there are the online ones (website, social media). Yet, despite all this easy availability and accessibility, it is not always easy to distinguish between real and fake, relevant and redundant, significant and inconsequential.

Updated Knowledge Lighthouse is a series meant for GenZ, that is, learners born after Y2K. The series covers 'classic' general knowledge content for learners of grades 1 to 8, but lays special emphasis on skills —learning skills, literacy skills and life skills— as well as knowledge gleaned from new learnings of the past few years, from COVID-19 to sustainability, from data science to global issues in an ever-shifting, ever-ephemeral, post-information world. All the new chapters, although dealing with topics of great gravity, are presented in an age-appropriate and friendly manner so as to kindle interest and lay the foundation for more in-depth learning.

A critical component of the Updated Knowledge Lighthouse books is the India content, wherein our country in all its complexity and diversity is presented through colourful, simple and exciting tasks, plus brand-new features such as state-focus, city-focus and visit-a-monument.

A particularly career-friendly inclusion in the Updated Knowledge Lighthouse series is Science, technology, engineering and mathematics (STEM), the disciplines of the future, and new global issues, presented under World Today. We hope to lighten these subjects for students, by adding a little sprinkle of trivia to them.

Sustainable development is one of the key phrases of this millennium, but what does it really mean for us, especially for children? The all-new Life on Land and Climate Action chapters not only sensitise learners but also encourage direct and immediate action.

In the Skills pages, the life skills section has tasks on safety and self-awareness. Connecting the dots is the foundation of knowledge and the series has chapters based on Higher Order Thinking Skills (HOTS) and critical thinking to train young minds to see patterns, learn to eliminate or choose details and observe better.

Become a Champion Quizzer

Updated Knowledge Lighthouse encourages all learners to be curious and explore the world around them. Those who observe and absorb all the time, learn from everyone and everything; they are the ones who become quizzers. Here are six rules that will help you become a champion quizzer.

1. Be curious—look around you, see everything, read everything.
2. Listen to others.
3. Seek out new experiences.
4. Learn to link events and people.
5. Do your own research and learn to spot fake news.
6. Remember, no matter how much you know, there is much more that you have yet to learn.

Now, go for it! We are sure that this series will expose a whole new generation of learners to the fun universe of general knowledge and enhance their love for learning and discovery.

~ Seema Chari and Kunal Savarkar

In this series ...

Updated Knowledge Lighthouse tasks are thematic and linear with visual, verbal, and strategic inputs to help students solve them and acquire knowledge through a wide range of subjects and themes.

World Around Us

22 Countries and Flags

Every country has a flag. Some flags look like one another. Colour these flags using the colour key.

1 Red 2 White 3 Blue 4 Green

World Around Us tasks take the learners on an exciting journey across the world.

Natural World

4 Animal Speech

Animals cannot talk. The sounds they make help other animals, and sometimes ever beings understand what they might be trying to say. Many common words are also u describe the sounds that animals make.

Fill in the blanks using the words given in the help box. Use the same word to fill blank and understand what sound that animal makes.

1 When it is cold, our teeth ....

2 On a computer, we select with the .... of a mouse.

Natural World section uncovers the magical realm of plants, animals and birds.

Clean Water and Sanitation

19 Saving Water and Soap

Earth is the only planet that has enough water to sustain life. So if we keep on wasting water, it will drain into the sea and our cities will run dry. Also, if too much soap or detergent goes into the soil or sea, a lot of animals can die from the chemicals. So, when we clean up or wash up, we should use water and soap carefully.

Match the wasteful actions in Column A with the better actions in Column B.

Column A: What many people do	Column B: What people should do instead

Sustainable Development Goals sensitises learners towards sustainable development of the planet.

India Focus

12 Respected Indians

These Indians are respected for their achievements.

Fill in the blanks using the words given in the help box. Each question has two

1 A former President of India, he is known as the .... Man of India. He was a scientist before he became the President.

A. P. J. Abdul Kalam

India Focus tasks are created to evoke a sense of wonder and pride in our nation.

Art and Entertainment

9 Monster Films

Children's films are not just about happy or cute things. They are about monsters and mean people too!

Read these story lines, look at the pictures and complete the names of the films. We have filled in the vowels, that is, a, e, i, o and u. You have to fill in the consonants.

1 A children's horror fiction series by RL Stine that has also been adapted as comics, films and TV series _OO_E_U_ _ _

2 A comic series and a film about a friendly ghost and his three nasty ghost uncles

Art and Entertainment tasks celebrate artists, artworks, paintings, movies, awards and achievements.

Sports

14 Ball Games

Find names of 10 common ball games in the word search and then write their names. The first letter of each sport is coloured to help you.

B	F	Z	N	Y	T	C	W	X	U	K	D	W
O	B	A	S	K	E	T	B	A	L	L	N	G
W	G	N	Q	W	N	V	I	Q	N	I	E	X
L	H	O	U	A	N	O	L	I	N	G	O	V
I	U	R	A	T	I	A	L	H	U	L	A	O
N	K	K	S	E	S	F	I	O	A	Y	M	L
G	W	E	H	M	G	C	A	C	Z	E	R	L

Sports section provides rules and records related to different sports.

Language and Literature

26 Interjections

Words that are used to express feelings such as joy, surprise or shock are called interjections. Sentences ending in interjections are followed by an exclamation mark (!).

Read the lines and choose the correct interjections from the help box and write them in the blanks provided.

1 2

Language and Literature tasks present vocabulary and etymology in a fun way.

World Today

19 Social Movemen[ts of] the 21st Century

As we mark the silver jubilee of this century, we can see that people of the twenty are more vocal than ever before, and members of every community have increasi a public voice through mass movements. Some of these are triggered by immedia while others have been simmering for a while before finding expression. Match th movements with their description and write the name of the country in which th

Name		Description
1 Jasmine Revolution/ Arab Spring	a	Led by social activist Anna Hazare, this 2011 movement saw protests across the country by citizens fighting against widespread corruption.
2 Schools Strike for Climate	b	This 2011 movement led to people talking about economic inequality and corporate greed; and the impact of wealth on law-making in the world's richest country.

World Today highlights the importance of understanding and addressing global challenges together.

Whiz fact

The Food Safety and Standards Authority of India (FSSAI) is an organisation that decides whether a food product is safe to consume. All packaged foods have an FSSAI licence number.

Whiz Fact is a spin-off fact about each topic or theme.

General Science

28 Famous Inventions

When something useful is made for the first time, it is called an invention. The person who makes an invention is called an inventor.

Read the clues and match the inventors to their inventions by writing letters in the boxes.

1 Orville Wright and Wilbur Wright

2 John Logie Baird

3 Thomas Alva Edison

General Science highlights some scientific achievements and provides facts for others.

Whiz quiz

Who invented these instruments?

1 Telescope ....

2 Camera ....

Whiz Quiz are fun activities that encourage self-learning.

21st Century Skills

21st century skills are necessary to succeed in the Age of Information. These skills are divided into three main sets, namely, learning skills, literacy skills and life skills.

Learning Skills

- Critical Thinking and HOTS
- Creativity
- Collaboration
- Communication

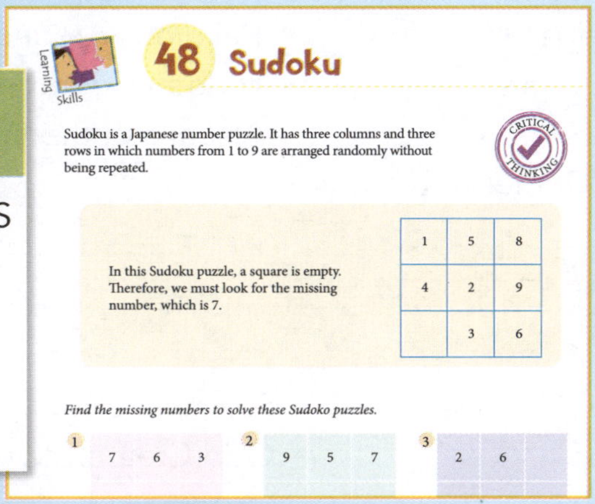

Learning Skills

48 Sudoku

Sudoku is a Japanese number puzzle. It has three columns and three rows in which numbers from 1 to 9 are arranged randomly without being repeated.

In this Sudoku puzzle, a square is empty. Therefore, we must look for the missing number, which is 7.

1	5	8
4	2	9
	3	6

Find the missing numbers to solve these Sudoko puzzles.

1. 7 6 3
2. 9 5 7
3. 2 6

Literacy Skills

- Technology
- Information
- Media
- Financial Literacy
- Data Handling

Literacy Skills

32 Fun with Wrappers

Every food product we buy has some information on its wrapper. Let us try to understand some terms or markings used on food wrappers.

Life Skills

- Problem-solving
- Self-awareness
- Safety
- Social Skills

Life Skills

44 Mind and Body

Write the names of these yoga poses using the words given in the help box.

1. ....
2. ....
3. ....

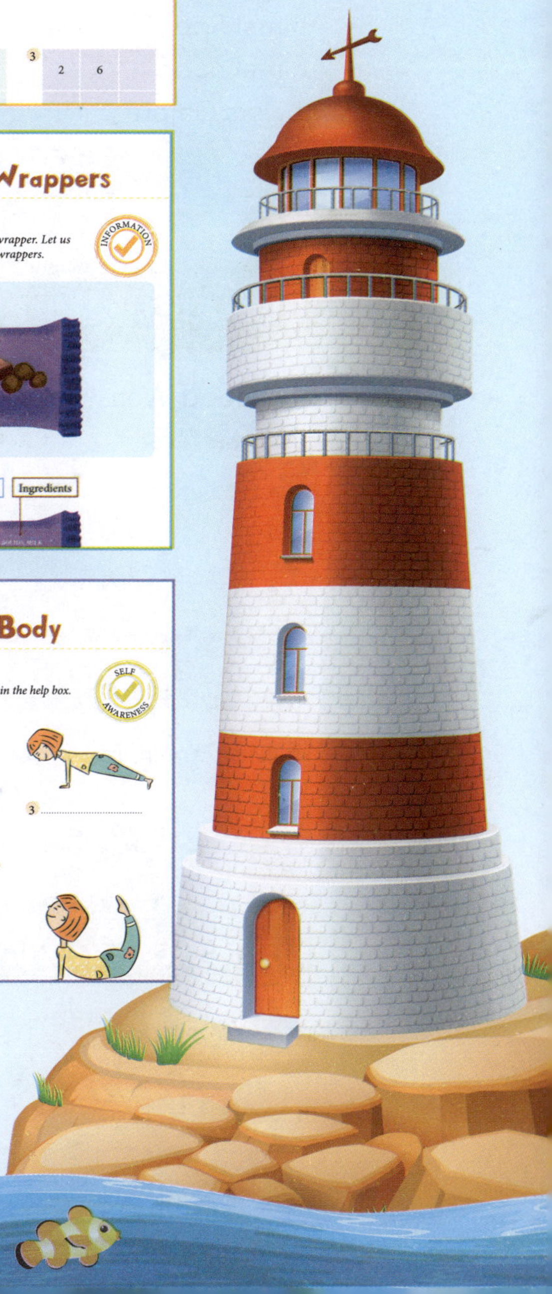

Detailed Contents

World Around Us

- Countries and Flags
- Countries and Capitals
- Going to America
- Sri Lanka, Here I Come!
- Religions Around the World
- Hidden Countries
- Oceans of the World

Natural World

- Animal Speech
- Animal Food
- Flowers Galore
- Sea Animals
- Odd Creature Out

Language and Literature

- What is the Good Word?
- Rhymes with Letters
- My Favourite Books
- Interjections

Art and Entertainment

- Monster Films

General Science

- Know Your Body
- Famous Inventions

India Focus

- Respected Indians
- Taj Mahal
- North, South, East, West
- Delhi
- India Extremes
- Northeast India
- Rabindranath Tagore

Sports

- Indoor Games
- Ball Games
- Sports Champions
- Athletic Fun
- Olympics Special

Sustainable Development Goals

- Be a Herb Farmer
- Saving Water and Soap
- Green Habits

Learning Skills

- Things Take Time
- Picture Puzzles
- Celestial Objects
- Anagrams
- Sudoku

Literacy Skills

- Colourful Edibles
- Control Key Shortcuts
- Notes on Notes
- Identity Cards
- Fun with Wrappers
- Closed Lists
- Space and Days

Life Skills

- Camping Time
- Being Safe
- Mind and Body

Contents

1	What is the Good Word?	9
2	Colourful Edibles	10
3	Rhymes with Letters	12
4	Animal Speech	14
5	Know Your Body	16
6	Be Herb Farmer	18
7	Animal Food	19
8	Indoor Games	20
9	Monster Films	21
10	Flowers Galore	22
11	My Favourite Books	24
12	Respected Indians	26
13	Sea Animals	28
14	Ball Games	30
15	Things Take Time	32
16	Camping Time	34
17	Taj Mahal	36
18	Control Key Shortcuts	37
19	Saving Water and Soap	38
20	Odd Creature Out	40
21	Sports Champions	42
22	Countries and Flags	44
23	Picture Puzzles	46
24	North, South, East, West	48
25	Notes on Notes	49
26	Interjections	50
27	Celestial Objects	52
28	Famous Inventions	54
29	Athletic Fun	56
30	Identity Cards	58
31	Countries and Capitals	59
32	Fun with Wrappers	60
33	Green Habits	62
34	Delhi	63
35	Closed Lists	64
36	Olympics Special	65
37	Space and Days	66
38	Going to America	67
39	Being Safe	68
40	India Extremes	70
41	Anagrams	71
42	Northeast India	72
43	Sri Lanka, Here I Come!	74
44	Mind and Body	75
45	Religions Around the World	76
46	Rabindranath Tagore	78
47	Hidden Countries	79
48	Sudoku	80
49	Oceans of the World	81
	Quiz Yourself 1	82
	Quiz Yourself 2	83
	Quiz Yourself 3	84
	Quiz Yourself 4	85
	Answer Key	86

1 What is the Good Word?

Some words sound the same but are spelled differently.

Fill in the blanks using the words given in the help box.

1

We took turns to skate, ... (a number) at a time.

2

The dog was sleeping so the cat .... (also) decided to sleep.

3

I can see the castle .... (not here).

4

The children are helping .... (his + her) mother.

5

.... (short for it is) a good day to stay home and read.

6

The dog kept wagging .... (belonging to it) tail.

Help box

It's	their	too	there	its	two

Whiz quiz

Sometimes two words can be joined to form shorter words. For example, 'what is' can be written as what's and 'you are' can be written as you're. A symbol called an apostrophe (') is used to indicate that one or more letters have been left out of a word.

Literacy Skills

2 Colourful Edibles

This basket is filled with colourful fruits and vegetables, which all have numbers. Their names are in the help box, but in broken parts! Join the parts to get the full names. Then, next to the correct numbers in the columns, write the names of fruits in the fruits column and the names of vegetables in the vegetables column.

DATA HANDLING

Whiz fact

Tomatoes are actually fruits of plants. They are the main ingredient of red pizza and pasta sauces.

Help box 1

WATER	MAN	PUMP	GIN	PAP
CAB	SPI	POT	CHE	BAN

Help box 2

GER	ATO	KIN	BAGE	GO
NACH	AYA	MELON	RRY	ANA

Answers:

	FRUITS		VEGETABLES
F1		V1	
F2		V2	
F3		V3	
F4		V4	
F5		V5	

Whiz quiz

1. Name a fruit which is eaten raw in salads.

   ....

2. Name a fruit that can be cooked.

   ....

3 Rhymes with Letters

One is a mouse, the plural is mice. What is common to Mickey, Stuart, Rémy and Jerry? They are all lovable characters in movies and stories, and they are all mice.

Now read this rhyme about a mouse.

Hickory dickory dock.

The mouse ran up the clock.

The clock struck one,

The mouse ran down,

Hickory dickory dock.

Let us write an acrostic poem. Each line should begin with the letters of the word 'mouse'. Here is an example.

M	y house
O	n the hill
U	sed to be
S	o full of mice
E	ek!

Now write acrostic poems using letters of the words 'tiger' and 'horse'.

1

T ....

I ....

G ....

E ....

R ....

2

H ....

O ....

R ....

S ....

E ....

Whiz fact

Walt Disney wanted to create a cartoon animal in place of Oswald The Lucky Rabbit. His new animal was none other than Mickey Mouse!

4 Animal Speech

Animals cannot talk. The sounds they make help other animals, and sometimes even human beings understand what they might be trying to say. Many common words are also used to describe the sounds that animals make.

Fill in the blanks using the words given in the help box. Use the same word to fill in the blank and understand what sound that animal makes.

1. When it is cold, our teeth ....

Monkeys ....

2. On a computer, we select with the .... of a mouse.

Dolphins ....

3. A .... is a musical instrument which produces a loud sound.

Elephants ....

4. A .... is a black bird.

Roosters ....

Whiz fact

Parrots and parakeets are talking birds. They can mimic the speech of human beings.

5 When stuck in a traffic jam, drivers often ....

Geese ....

6 The outside of a tree trunk is called ....

Dogs ....

7 When someone cracks a joke, we ....

Hyenas ....

8 When a nice song plays, we .... along.

Whales ....

9 When door hinges are not oiled, they ....

Mice ....

10 When we try to sing with a sore throat, we ....

Frogs ....

Help box

trumpet | click | bark | chatter | honk
sing | crow | laugh | squeak | croak

Whiz fact

Name the animals that make these sounds.

1 Bray ....

2 Mew ....

General Science

5 Know Your Body

A rebus is a puzzle that has pictures for words or parts of words.

Solve these rebus puzzles to find the names of different parts of the body.

1 We are hard and give your body shape. You cannot see us because we are covered in muscles and skin.

 – **W** +  – **T** = ...

2 I am a bit larger than your fist. I pump blood through your body.

 – **N** + 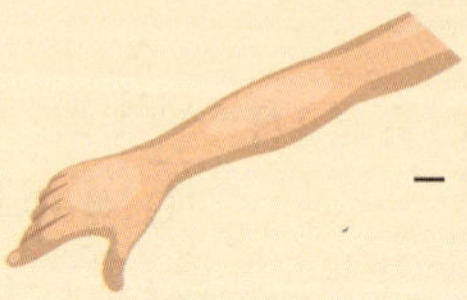 – **M** + **T** = ...

3 I am inside your head and look like a shelled walnut. I help you to think and learn.

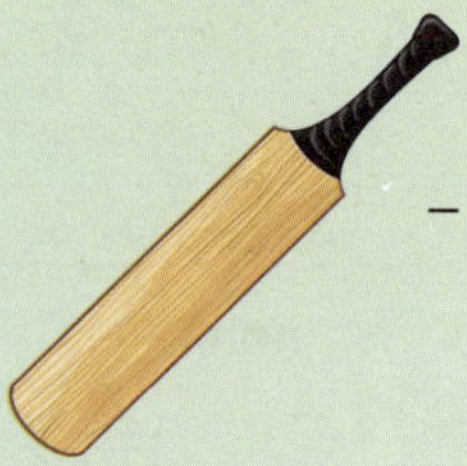 – **AT** +  = ...

Whiz fact

The bony case in which our brain and sense organs are enclosed is called the skull. It is made up of 22 bones which are joined together.

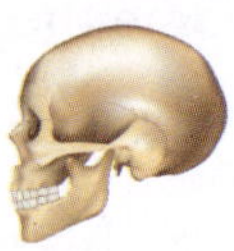

4 I am the largest organ in the body and I am very thin.

 - **Y** + 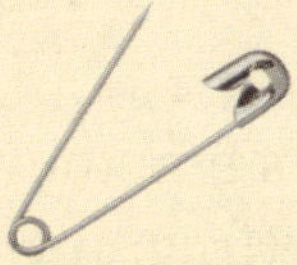 - **P** = ...

5 I am curved and help you stand straight.

 - **OON** + ______ - **L** = ...

6 Once you swallow food, it reaches me. I help you digest the food and give you energy.

 - **OL** +  - **P** +  - **AIR**

= ....

7 We are a pair and help you to breathe. The air you take in reaches us.

 - **CH** +  - **OAT** + **S**

= ....

Whiz quiz

Which is the only bone of the skull that can move? ....

Life on Land

6 Be a Herb Farmer

Herbs are plants that do not have a woody stem; they are soft, green and leafy. Herbs may be medicinal or aromatic (fragrant). Along with spices, they add flavour, aroma and texture to our food. They are extremely healthy too! *Use these rebuses (pictures and letters) and descriptions to guess the names of some common herbs.*

Rebus	Use	Herb
1.  – NE +  – NG + A+  – THU	Used as a garnish on foods and as an ingredient in chutney	i Mint
2.  – Y + S+  – GR – L	Chewed as leaves, torn and served on pizza and blended to make pesto sauce	ii Curry
3.  – LK +  – A	Chewed as leaves, used as a garnish and as an ingredient in chutney or sauce	iii Lemongrass
4.  – T +  – LO	Used fresh in gravies, with vegetables, in sambar, etc., or blended into chutney	iv Basil
5.  + 	Used in Thai curries, but also in mosquito repellent!	v Coriander

Whiz activity

It is easy to grow a herb garden, even if you live in a small house or flat. Follow these simple steps:

1. Take a foot-deep, narrow container, place it on a windowsill. The container should have holes in the base and a plate below it (for excess water).
2. Cut out a piece of jute cloth and place it on the base of the container, to keep pests away.
3. Fill the container with soil. You can ask a gardener for herb-friendly soil. A good combination is topsoil + compost + sand. Then, with gloves on, mix up the soil with your hands.
4. Sow seeds of some herbs. Plant herbs like coriander, basil and parsley in the centre of your container, and oregano, rosemary and thyme on the outer edges of your container.
5. Watch your garden grow, snip off the freshest herbs and add them to your food!

7 Animal Food

Carnivorous comes from *carne*, meaning flesh, and *vorare*, meaning to eat or devour. Herbivorous comes from *herb*, meaning plant, and *vorare*, meaning to eat or devour. Omnivorous comes from *omni*, meaning everything, and *vorare*, meaning to eat or devour.

Look at the pictures and read the lines about them. Write C if the animal is carnivorous, H if it is herbivorous and O if it is omnivorous.

Picture	Lines	C/H/O
1 	 A horse eats hay, grass and oats.	....
2 	 A lion eats animal flesh.	....
3 	 A fox eats chickens, mice, fruit, eggs or plants.	....
4 	 A monkey eats fruit, insects or anything you leave out.	....
5 	 A cow eats grass, leaves and vegetable peels.	....
6 	 A lizard eats insects.	....
7 	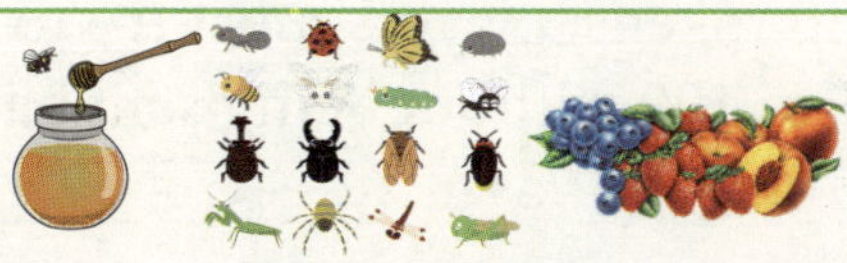 A bear eats honey, insects and fruit.	....
8 	 A dog eats meat and bones, rice, bread and any dairy product.	....

Sports

8 Indoor Games

When it rains or is too hot, just sit with your family or friends and play a game at home! Here are some easy and fun games.

Look at the pictures, read the lines about them and then write their names using the help box.

Games		Description	Name of the game
1		This game for 4 players has fun tokens and squares like Go, Chance, Community Chest and Jail. It takes a long time to play.	....
2		This game has a lot of coloured plastic blocks that can be joined together to build lots of things.	....
3		Letter tiles are used to make words and placed on the boards squares. Some squares offer double or triple points for letters or words.	....
4		This simple game for 2 to 4 players uses a board divided into 4 sections. Each player has 4 tokens that all need to reach HOME.	....
5		This game has a bunch of wooden tiles that must be stacked up to form a tower. If the tower falls, you lose!	....
6		This game for 2 to 4 players tests your aim. A striker is used to hit 9 black or white coins and a red-coloured 'queen'.	....
7		The classic black-and-white square game board and 16 tokens per player add up to a very popular and brainy game.	....
8		Using a die and tokens, players must try to climb from square 1 to 100 without being sent back down by snakes!	....

Help box

Jenga · Scrabble · Monopoly · Ludo · Carrom · Lego · Battleship · Chess · Snakes and Ladders

Art and Entertainment

9 Monster Films

Children's films are not just about happy or cute things. They are about monsters and mean people too!

Read these story lines, look at the pictures and complete the names of the films. We have filled in the vowels, that is, a, e, i, o and u. You have to fill in the consonants.

1 A children's horror fiction series by RL Stine that has also been adapted as comics, films and TV series

_OO_E_U_ _ _

2 A comic series and a film about a friendly ghost and his three nasty ghost uncles

_A_ _E_

3 A movie about Dracula, his daughter, lots of monsters and one human

_O_E_ _ _A_ _ _ _ _ A_ IA

4 A movie based on a Roald Dahl book, featuring Luke and his grandmother

_ _E _I_ _ _E_

5 A movie about a wicked fairy who is also a fairy godmother; she places a curse on a young princess

_A_E_I_E_ _

Whiz fact

Count Dracula is a character based on a real person who lived in Romania. Thanks to Bram Stoker's novel by the same name *Dracula* in the 15th century, the blood-sucking vampire became a huge and scary villain.

10 Flowers Galore

Flowers are used for more than just decoration.

Read the clues and look at the pictures. Write the names of these flowers using words from the help box and reading the hints.

1 This fragrant flower is called *champa* in Hindi. It is used for making perfume and incense sticks.

....

Hint: This long word ends with the Hindi word for 'water'.

2 This flower is also known as *moringa*. We eat a long stick-like vegetable that grows on its plant.

....

Hint: This word is made up of a musical instrument and something to hit it with.

3 This flower grows on a huge tree that gives us shade.

....

Hint: The first part of this word is almost a large sea bird and rhymes with 'pull'.

4 Poets have written many poems on this beautiful flower. It closes in the night and grows mostly in mountainous regions.

....

Hint: The first part of this word rhymes with the sound word 'paf!', and the second part of this word is the Hindustani word for 'heart'.

5 They are small, roundish flowers that grow in bunches. They are pink, violet and even dark blue.

....

Hint: This word sounds like 'fancy'.

6 This flower is used as a spice. It also gives us oil.

....

Hint: This word rhymes with 'stove'.

7 This flower can be pink, purple or even white. It grows in huge bushes. We often see it growing on walls.

....

Hint: This long name has a middle part which means 'to win or earn something'.

8 This red or white flower is used as tea. It is also used for decoration.

....

Hint: This word rhymes with 'discuss'.

Help box

pansy | frangipani | bougainvillea | drumstick flower | daffodil | hibiscus | *gulmohar* flower | clove flower

Whiz fact

Flowers such as sunflowers and daisies are composite flowers. They are made up of many tiny flowers that appear like a single flower.

Language and Literature

11 My Favourite Books

Write the names of the books with the help of the clues. Take one word from each help box and join them to find the names of some popular children's books.

1 Mowgli is brought up by a wolf pack.
The ....

2 A girl falls into a rabbit hole.
.... *Adventures in* ....

3 A man travels to the land of tiny people.
....

4 A mouse is adopted by a family.
....

5 A bear whose best friend is a piglet.
.... *-the-* ....

Help box 1

Alice's	*Charlotte's*	*Black*	*Gulliver's*	*Winnie*
Pippi	*Bear*	*Stuart*	*Jungle*	*Peter*

6 A spider is the heroine of this book.

....

7 This little boy could fly but never grew up.

....

8 A nine-year-old girl lives with her pet monkey and pet horse in a little Swedish village.

....

9 A bear from Darkest Peru moves in with a family in London.

A .... *Called* ....

10 A horse tells the story of its life.

....

Help box 2

Pan	*Travels*	*Web*	*Little*	*Paddington*
Longstocking	*Beauty*	*Book*	*Pooh*	*Wonderland*

Whiz fact

A Little Pretty Pocket-Book written by John Newbery is considered the first modern children's book. It is a mix of rhymes, picture stories and games.

India Focus

12 Respected Indians

These Indians are respected for their achievements.

Fill in the blanks using the words given in the help box. Each question has two answers.

1 A former President of India, he was known as the .... Man of India. He was a scientist before he became the President.

A. P. J. Abdul Kalam

Anandibai Gopalrao Joshi

2 Married at the age of 9, she was supported by her husband to become a doctor. She studied .... in the US and became India's first woman physician.

3 She was a classical dancer who set up an academy for arts called Kalakshetra. She learnt .... from the famous Russian dancer, Anna Pavlova.

Rukmini Devi Arundale

Dhyan Chand

4 One of the greatest hockey players of India, he won three Olympic .... medals. His birthday is celebrated as the National Sports Day in India.

5 Also known as the .... of India, she was a famous freedom fighter and a poet. She was born in present-day Telangana.

Sarojini Naidu

Jawaharlal Nehru

6 He was the first Prime Minister of India. His birthday is celebrated as ....

7 This leader was the first Vice President of India. He also won the Bharat Ratna. In his honour, we celebrate his birthday as .... Day.

Sarvepalli Radhakrishnan

Lata Mangeshkar

8 This Queen of .... was one of the greatest Indian playback singers ever. This Bharat Ratna singer sang for over seventy years before dying of COVID-19 in February 2022.

Help box

medicine	Children's Day	Missile	gold
Nightingale	Teachers'	melody	ballet

Whiz fact

Sardar Vallabhbhai Patel is known as the Iron Man of India. He is regarded as one of the most important leaders of India's freedom struggle.

Natural World

13 Sea Animals

Fill in the blanks with the names of some sea animals given in the help box.

1 An .... has eight limbs.

2 A .... has a water spout on its head.

3 A...................................... has five arms and looks like a star.

4 A...................................... has a head and many long wavy tentacles.

Whiz fact

Creatures living in the sea breathe through gills. Whales and dolphins come to the surface of water to breathe and then go back in the water.

5 A .... is tiny. Its head looks like a horse's head and it has a curvy curled-up tail.

6 A .... is a very big fish with many sharp teeth.

7 An .... has two shells. Sometimes it makes pearls.

8 A .... has two huge claws and many pointy legs.

Help box

shark	octopus	oyster	seahorse
whale	crab	jellyfish	starfish

Sports

14 Ball Games

Find names of 10 common ball games in the word search and then write their names. The first letter of each sport is coloured to help you.

B	F	Z	N	Y	T	C	W	X	U	K	D	W
O	B	A	S	K	E	T	B	A	L	L	N	G
W	G	N	Q	W	N	V	I	Q	N	I	E	X
L	H	O	U	A	N	O	L	I	N	G	O	V
I	U	R	A	T	I	A	L	H	U	L	A	O
N	K	K	S	E	S	F	I	O	A	Y	M	L
G	W	E	H	M	G	C	A	C	Z	E	R	L
G	T	L	L	S	O	U	R	K	B	Y	R	E
O	B	L	N	K	W	Y	D	E	I	Y	U	Y
L	Q	I	L	A	C	K	S	Y	O	S	G	B
F	I	N	W	I	N	D	S	U	R	F	B	A
N	N	G	K	N	Y	M	P	H	E	T	Y	L
P	O	L	O	G	A	R	I	S	O	N	E	L

1 

....

2 

....

3 

....

4 

....

5

....

6

....

7

....

8

....

9

....

10

....

Whiz quiz

Which of these is a popular bat-and-ball game of America?

a baseball   b tennis   c hockey

Whiz fact

Lacrosse is a stick and ball game. The head of the stick has a net which is used to carry, pass or throw the ball into the goal. Lacrosse was first played in Canada.

Learning Skills

15 Things Take Time

CRITICAL THINKING

Read the starting time and the finishing time of the activities on the clocks and write how much time it took to do each activity.

1 Riya started brushing her teeth at 7:24 a.m. and finished at 7:26 a.m.

.... hours .... minutes

2 The storm began at 12:35 p.m. and ended at 2:20 p.m.

.... hours .... minutes

3 The movie started at 11:45 a.m. and ended at 1:55 p.m.

.... hours .... minutes

4 The birthday party started at 5:50 p.m. and ended at 9:00 p.m.

.... hours .... minutes

5 The train started from Nagpur at 8:40 p.m. and arrived in Mumbai next day at 8:05 a.m.

.... hours .... minutes

6 The quiz began at 9:10 a.m. and ended at 10:30 a.m.

.... hours .... minutes

7 The hike began at 8:40 a.m. and ended at 10:05 a.m.

.... hours .... minutes

Whiz fact

An hourglass or a sandglass can be used to measure time. It has two glass bulbs with a narrow 'neck' in between.

Life Skills

16 Camping Time

PROBLEM SOLVING

Tick (✓) the things you will need to pack for a 3-day camp and cross the things you will not need.

1

2

3

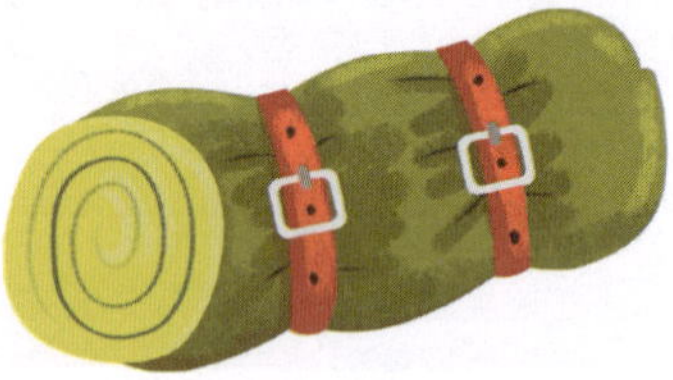

4

5

6

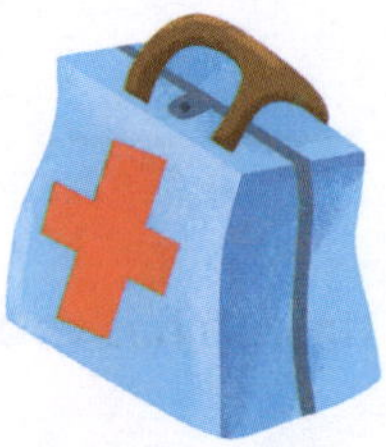

7

8

18

17

16

15

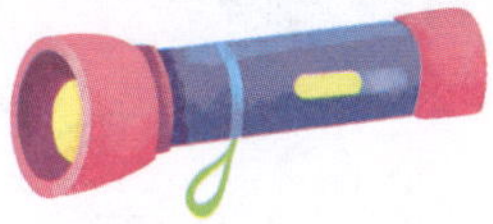

14

13

12

9

10

11

India Focus

17 Taj Mahal

Complete the sentences about the Taj Mahal using the words given in the help box.

1 The Taj Mahal is a ...., which means a building that houses tombs.

2 It is located on the banks of the river .... in the city of Agra in Uttar Pradesh.

3 It was built using white .... from Makrana.

4 It has a huge onion-shaped ....

5 The Taj Mahal has four tall ....

6 It is surrounded by four lovely .... with water channels.

Help box

dome	minarets	Yamuna	mausoleum	marble	gardens

Whiz fact

The Taj Mahal was built by the Mughal emperor Shah Jahan for his wife, Mumtaz Mahal.

18 Control Key Shortcuts

Each button of a computer keyboard is called a key. The Control keys or the Ctrl keys are at the bottom of the keyboard. Pressing the Ctrl key and N together allows us to open a new file. This shortcut can be written as Ctrl + N.

Using the help box, write the commands these control key shortcuts are used for.

1. Ctrl + S ....
2. Ctrl + X ....
3. Ctrl + C ....
4. Ctrl + V ....
5. Ctrl + Z ....
6. Ctrl + Y ....
7. Ctrl + P ....
8. Ctrl + W ....

Help box

close file | save file | cut | undo | paste | print | copy | redo

Whiz fact

The shortcut Ctrl + A is used to select all text in a document. All these shortcuts work on a Windows system

19 Saving Water and Soap

Earth is the only planet that has enough water to sustain life. So if we keep on wasting water, it will drain into the sea and our cities will run dry. Also, if too much soap or detergent goes into the soil or sea, a lot of animals can die from the chemicals. So, when we clean up or wash up, we should use water and soap carefully.

Match the wasteful actions in Column A with the better actions in Column B. Write the correct answer in the space provided in Column A.

Column A: What many people do	Column B: What people should do instead
1  Take a shower ☐	a  Fill the glass to half and use undrunk water to water plants
2 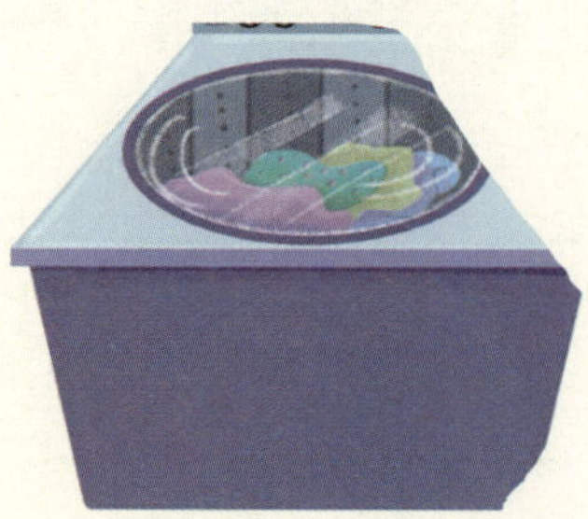 Wash 2-3 clothing items in the washing machine ☐	b  Rinse dishes immediately after use; it will take less water to wash them later

3

Leave dirty dishes in the sink; somebody will wash them at one go

4

Leave plates with leftover food in them in the sink

5

Ask for a glass of water, drink a little and throw the rest away

6

Rinse clothes or dishes under running water

c

Wash a full load in the washing machine

d

Rinse clothes or dishes in a sink with the drain plugged

e

Scrape leftover food off dishes before leaving them for washing

f

Bathe using a bucket and mug

Natural World

20 Odd Creature Out

Circle the odd one in each row. With the help of the hints write why it is the odd one out.

1

a 
Penguin

b 
Kingfisher

c 
Sparrow

d 
Eagle

It is odd because ....

Hint: What do most birds do?

2

a 
Shark

b 
Cat

c 
Crocodile

d 
Frog

It is odd because ....

Hint: Where do these animals live?

3

a 
Snake

b 
Monkey

c 
Lizard

d 
Chameleon

It is odd because ....

Hint: What kind of skin do these animals have?

4 a

Lion fish

b

Dolphin

c

Whale

d

Goldfish

It is odd because ....

Hint: How do these animals breathe?

5 a

Ant

b

Bee

c

Cockroach

d

Spider

It is odd because ....

Hint: How many legs do these insects have?

6 a

Lobster

b

Crab

c

Prawn

d

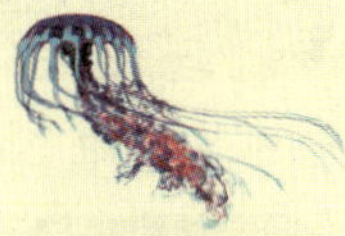

Jellyfish

It is odd because ....

Hint: What kind of body do these animals have?

Whiz fact

Mammals are animals that give birth to their young ones. Monkeys, lions and human beings are mammals. Duck-billed platypus and spiny anteaters found in Australia are mammals whose babies hatch from eggs.

Sports

21 Sports Champions

Look at the pictures and complete the names of the these sports champions play. The help box has words that form part of the name of the sport. Each sport is represented by two champions.

Leander Peas

1 ....ING

Sania Mirza

Sakshi Malik

2 W........ ....ING

Ravi Kumar Dahiya

Saina Nehwal

3 ....MINTON

P.V. Sindhu

Mithali Raj

4 C........ ....ET

Bhuvneshwar Kumar

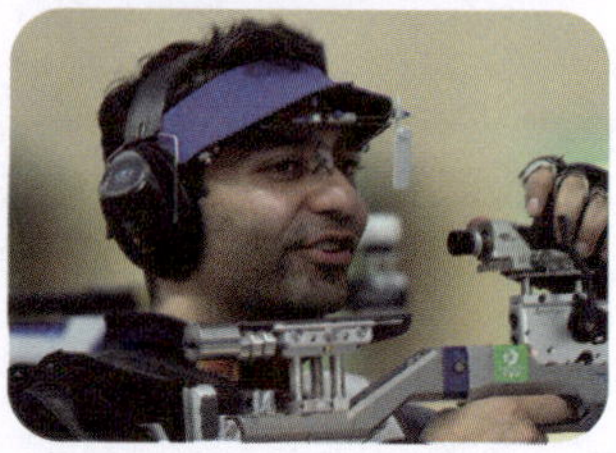

Abhinav Bindra

5 S........ ....ING

Anjali Bhagwat

Viswanathan Anand

6 C........ ....SS

Rameshbabu Praggnanandhaa

Anirban Lahiri

7 ....LF

Aditi Ashok

Mary Kom

8 ....ING

Vijender Singh

Help box

Go | Ten | Bad | rest | he | Box | hoot | rick

Whiz fact

The highest sporting honour awarded in India is the Major Dhyan Chand Khel Ratna. It used to be called the Rajiv Gandhi Khel Ratna. The first sportsperson to receive it was Vishwanathan Anand.

Whiz quiz

Which sportspersons were awarded the Major Dhyan Chand Khel Ratna in 2023?

22 Countries and Flags

Every country has a flag. Some flags look like one another. Colour these flags using the colour key.

(1) Red (2) White (3) Blue (4) Green

1

France

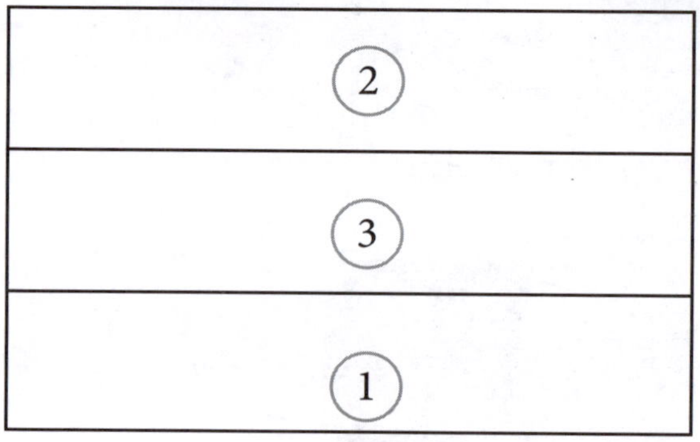

Russia

2

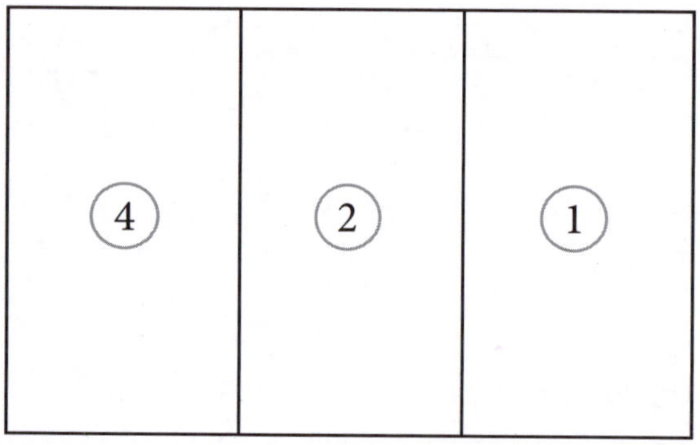

Italy

Hungary

3 

Japan

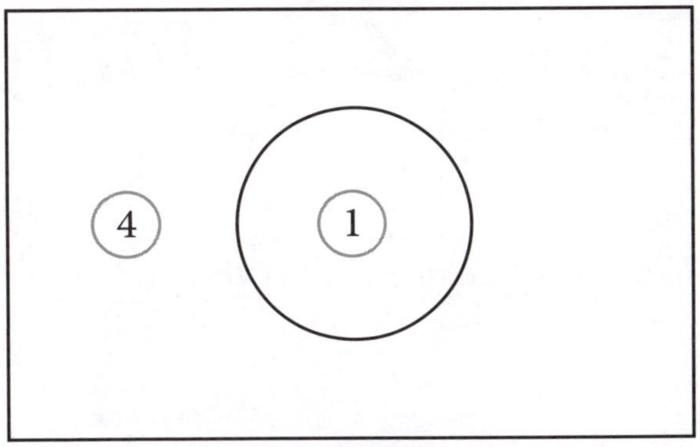

Bangladesh

4 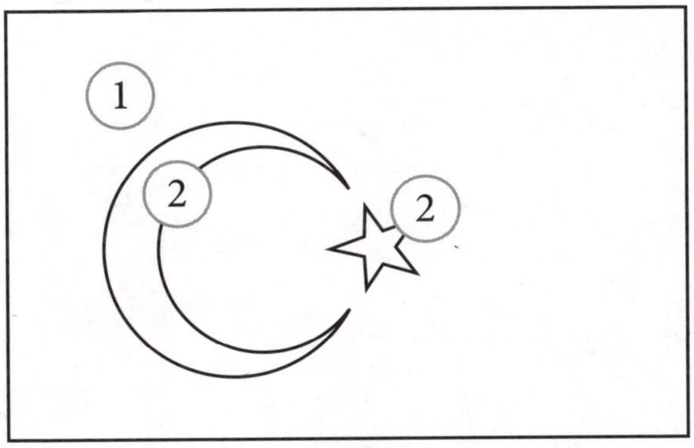

Turkey

Pakistan

5 

Poland

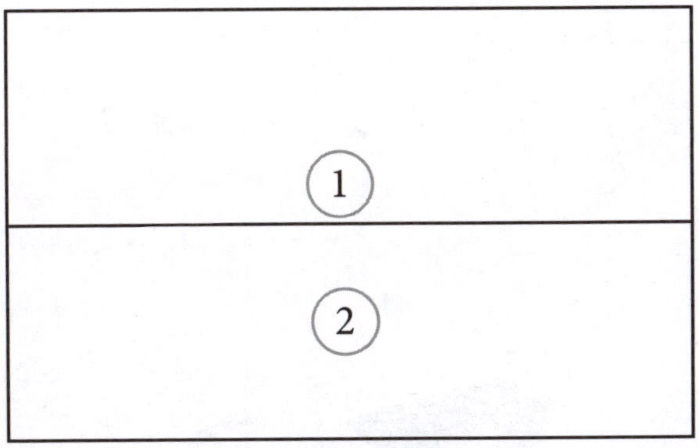

Indonesia

Whiz fact

Most flags are rectangular. The flag of Nepal is the only one which looks like two triangles placed on top of one another.

Learning Skills

23 Picture Puzzles

CRITICAL THINKING

Label these pictures to solve these rebus puzzles. One has been done for you.

1  +  = 

Cup .... Cake .... Cupcake

2  - T +  = 

....

3 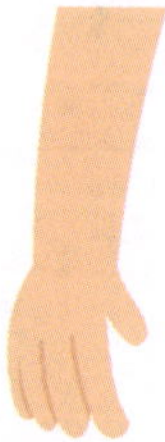 +  = 

....

4  - S +  = 

....

5  + B +  = 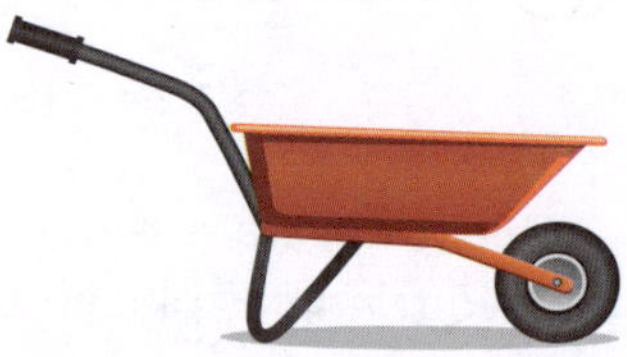

....

6  +  = 

....

7  - ET + 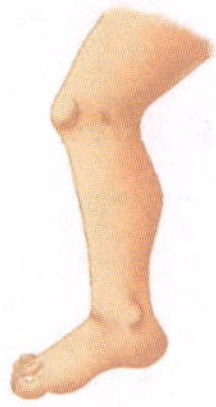 - G = 

....

8  + 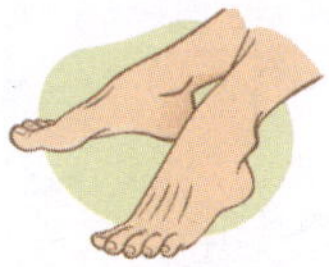 - FE = 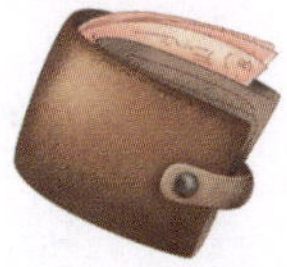

....

9  +  - T = 

....

10 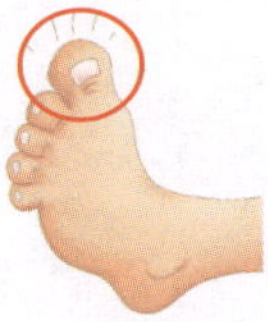 - E + A +  - AR = 

....

Whiz fact

Rebuses can be quite complicated. Rebus M ce, M ce, M ce means 'Three Blind Mice'. This is because I's are missing from the words or 'no eyes'!

24 North, South, East, West

India Focus

Have you seen a compass? The needle of a compass always points to the north. If we face north, the south is right behind us. The east is on our right and the west is on our left.

Look at the map of India. Some of the states have been coloured. Write whether these states are in the north, south, east, west or in the centre of India.

1 ....

2 ....

3 ....

4 ....

5 ....

Whiz fact

The largest state in India is Rajasthan and the smallest state is Goa.

Literacy Skills

25 Notes on Notes

FINANCIAL LITERACY

The currency of India is the rupee.

Match the colours to the notes and write the names of the emblems on these bank notes. One has been done for you.

1

Konark Sun Temple c

2

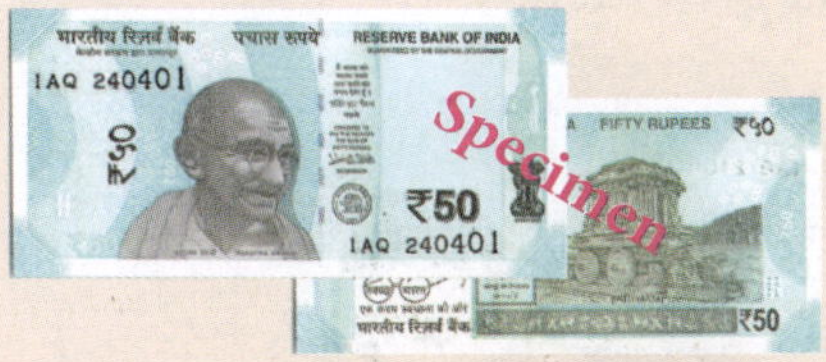

.... [ ]

3

.... [ ]

4

.... [ ]

5

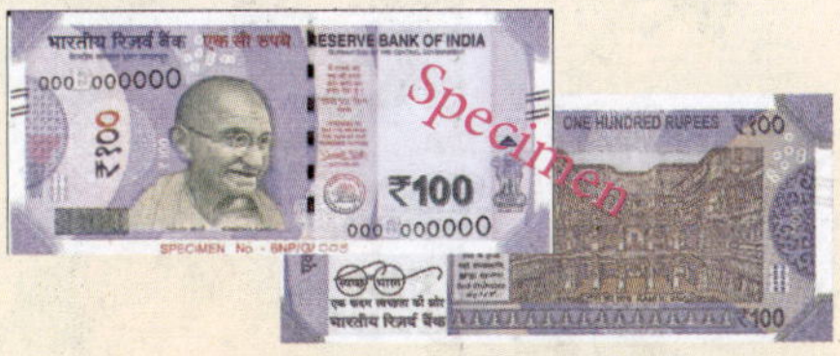

.... [ ]

6

.... [ ]

Colours

a Magenta

b Bright yellow

c Chocolate brown

d Fluorescent blue

e Lavender

f Stone Grey

Help box

Sanchi Stupa | Mangalyaan | Rani Ki Vav | Konark Sun Temple | Hampi with Chariot | Red Fort

26 Interjections

Words that are used to express feelings such as joy, surprise or shock are called interjections. Sentences ending in interjections are followed by an exclamation mark (!).

Read the lines and choose the correct interjections from the help box and write them in the blanks provided.

1

A book fell right on your toe.

....

2

You show a beautiful drawing you made to your family.

....

3

You have just seen a lizard in your soup.

....

4

Your mom had promised you a treat but she has just cancelled it.

....

Whiz fact

Every language has its own interjections. In French and Italian, people yell *ayi-ayi-ayi-ayi*! when hurt.

5

Your parents just told you that they have booked tickets for a movie.

....

6

Your friend's father calls up to tell you that she has fallen sick.

....

7

Your friend has just done a headstand.

....

8

You are with your friend inside a library and she is talking noisily.

....

Help box

yahoo! eek! wow! shh! boo-hoo! ouch! ta-da! oh no!

Whiz quiz

Find matching interjections in your language for the ones given in this chapter.

27 Celestial Objects

Learning Skills

CRITICAL THINKING

Using the letter code and the clues, find out the names of the planets of the solar system.

A = ©	M = ɟ	S = ★	C = §	N = ⌘	E = ∞
O = ⓘ	U = ⏎	H = ♦	P = ⏏	J = ⊘	R = ≅
Y = ⌥	I = ^	T = •	V = ≥		

1 The smallest planet of solar system, it is named after a Roman God of the same name.

ɟ	∞	≅	§	⏎	≅	⌥

2 This planet is known as the 'morning star' or the 'evening star'. The Sun rises in the west and sets in the east on this planet.

≥	∞	⌘	⏎	★

3 This is the only planet known to have life on it.

∞	©	≅	•	♦

Whiz fact

Celestial objects, which means objects in the sky or space, that move around the planets are called satellites. The moon is the satellite of the planet Earth.

4 Also called the 'red planet', it is the neighbour of the only planet that has life on it. India's space probe called Mangalyaan landed on its surface in 2014.

ɿ	©	≅	★

5 The largest planet in the solar system, it is named after the Roman sky god.

⃠	⏎	⏏	^	•	∞	≅

6 This planet has rings around it that can be seen at night without a telescope. A day of the week is named after it.

★	©	•	⏎	≅	⌘

7 Also known as the 'ice giant', it is not the farthest planet from the Sun and yet has the coldest temperature in the solar system.

⏎	≅	©	⌘	⏎	★

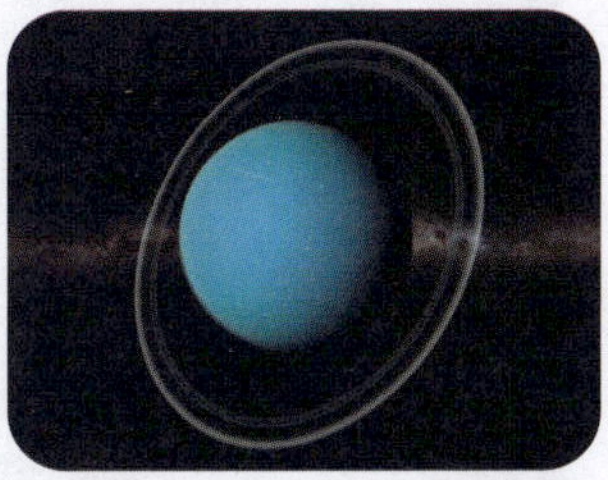

8 This planet is blue in colour and named after the Roman god of the sea.

⌘	∞	⏏	•	⏎	⌘	∞

28 Famous Inventions

When something useful is made for the first time, it is called an invention. The person who makes an invention is called an inventor.

Read the clues and match the inventors to their inventions by writing letters in the boxes.

1 

Orville Wright and Wilbur Wright

2 

John Logie Baird

3 

Thomas Alva Edison

4 

Alexander Graham Bell and Antonio Meucci

5 

Charles Babbage

Whiz fact

The Chinese were great inventors. They invented paper, clocks and the compass.

a

Television

b

Aeroplane

Clues

1. The Wright Brothers wondered how humans could fly.
2. John Logie Baird tried to find a way to watch programmes at home.
3. Thomas Alva Edison helped us have light even after sunset.
4. Alexander Graham Bell and Antonio Meucci found out how to make sound travel from one place to the other.
5. Charles Babbage invented a machine which allowed all kinds of calculations.

c

Telephone

e

Bulb

d

Computer

Whiz quiz

Who invented these instruments?

1. Telescope ....

2. Camera ....

Sports

29 Athletic Fun

Athletics are sports that include running, jumping, throwing or walking.

Read the clues and write the names of these athletic sports in the crossword puzzle using the words given in the help box.

Whiz fact

Steeplechase is an obstacle race that was first played in Ireland. The obstacles used in this foot race include water streams, ditches and fences.

Across

4 A competition in which a long spear is thrown as far as possible

5 A race between two or more teams, each member of the team runs one section of the race

6 A competition in which a metal ball attached to a steel wire is flung as far as possible

7 A long-distance race of a little more than 42 km

8 A leap as far away as possible from a take off point

9 A competition in which a heavy metal ball is pushed into the air as far as possible

Down

1 A competition in which a heavy disc-shaped object is flung as far as possible

2 A race in which runners jump over obstacles

3 An athletics event in which athletes jump over a high bar, using a long flexible pole to help lift themselves up

Help box

marathon | javelin throw | hurdles | hammer throw | relay | shot put | discus throw | pole vault | long jump

Whiz quiz

How many athletic events make a decathlon?

Literacy Skills

30 Identity Cards

Read the sentences and write the names of these identity cards using the words given in the help box.

INFORMATION

1 An identity card that allows a person to drive. It has a person's photograph and a unique number.

....

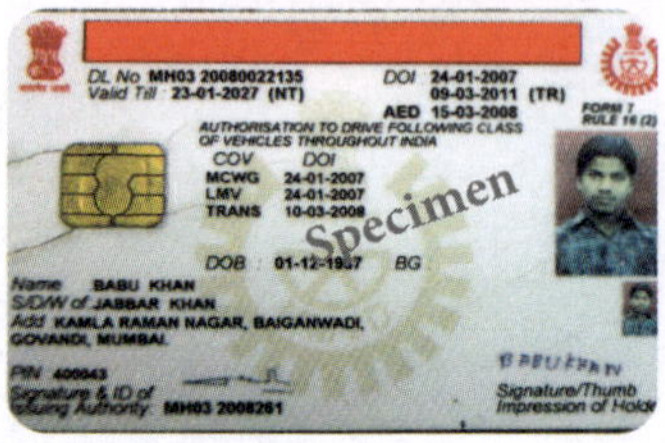

2 A booklet that allows us to travel to a different country. It has a unique number which is a combination of letters and numbers.

....

3 An identity card that allows a person to vote in elections in India.

....

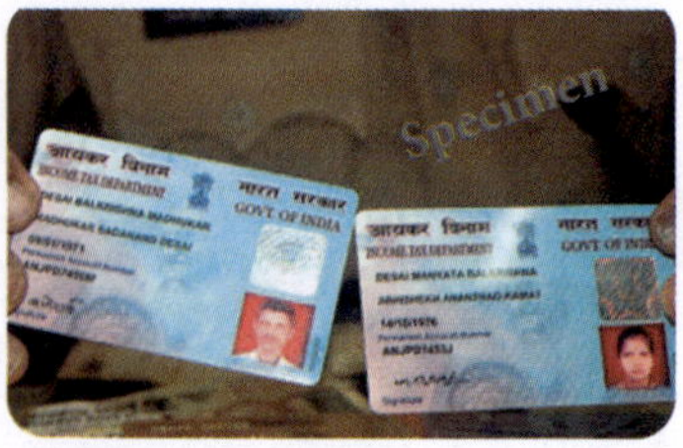

4 An identity card issued by the Income Tax Department of India. It has a ten-character code which is a combination of letters and numbers.

....

Help box

Voter ID	PAN Card	Passport	Driving licence

Whiz quiz

List 4 things mentioned in your school identity card.

1 .... 2 ....

3 .... 4 ....

31 Countries and Capitals

Here are the six biggest countries in the world with their capitals. Some letters are missing either from the name of the country or the capital. Read the clues and complete the names of these countries and capitals. Each country-capital pair has two blanks that should be filled with the same letters.

1. Russia

The .... gives us milk.

Mos........ ....

2. ....ada

Soft drinks come in a bottle or a ....

Ottawa

3. B........ ....zil

.... is an Egyptian god with a very short name.

B........ ....silia

4. United States of America

If our clothes are dirty, we .... them.

....ington D.C.

5. ....a

Below our lips is our ....

Beijing

6. Australia

A three-letter word which means 'to make a mistake' ....

Canb........ ....a

Whiz fact

India is the seventh largest country in the world by area, and the largest in the world by population. During colonial rule, Calcutta (now Kolkata) was the capital of British India, but in 1911, the capital shifted to New Delhi, which remains the capital to date.

32 Fun with Wrappers

Every food product we buy has some information on its wrapper. Let us try to understand some terms or markings used on food wrappers.

INFORMATION

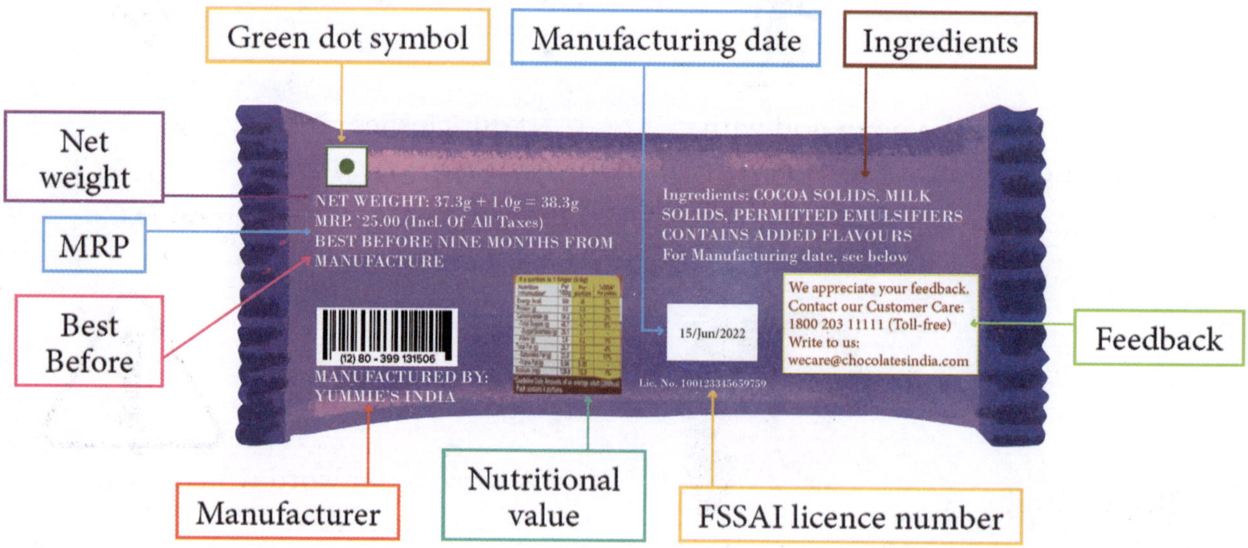

Whiz fact

The Food Safety and Standards Authority of India (FSSAI) is an organisation that decides whether a food product is safe to consume. All packaged foods have an FSSAI licence number.

Complete this crossword using the clues about information given on a chocolate wrapper.

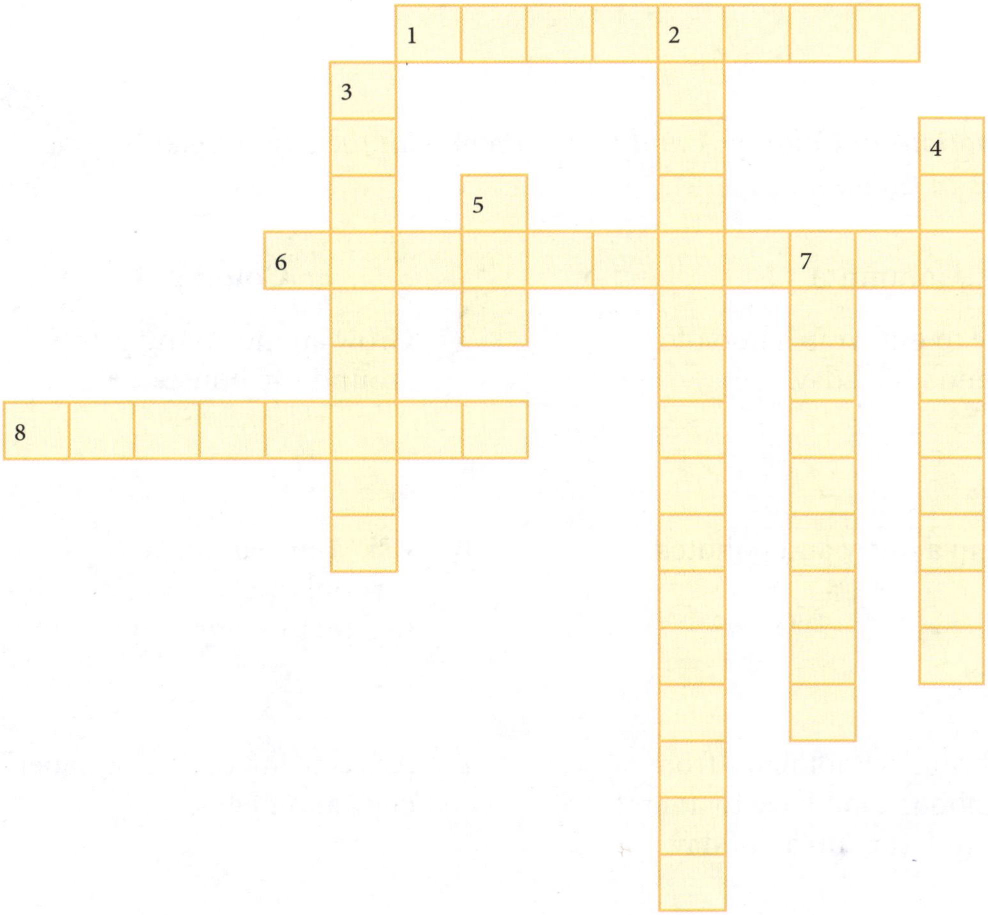

Across

1 The food product is fully vegetarian (5, 3)

6 List of food items used to make the product (11)

8 Complaints, suggestions or something nice to say about the product (8)

Down

2 Important nutrients present in the food product (11, 5)

3 Name of the food product and the company that makes it (5, 4)

4 Date before which the product must be eaten (4, 6)

5 Highest price a buyer must pay for the product (3)

7 Total weight of the product in the packet (3, 6)

Climate Action

33 Green Habits

Read these situations in Column A and match them with the environment-friendly actions in Column B.

Column A	Column B
1 You have to gift wrap a book for your friend's birthday.	a Grow air-purifying plants around the house.
2 You live in a dusty and polluted place.	b Ask your parents to organise a carpool or else travel to school together by bus.
3 You and your schoolmates from the neighbourhood have to attend a school function on a holiday.	c Avoid using plastic or paper cups and plates.
4 You need to buy bread and milk from a store.	d Use old newspapers and decorate them with colours and ribbons.
5 You are planning to invite your school friends to your house for a party.	e Carry a cloth bag while shopping.

India Focus

34 Delhi

New Delhi is the capital of India. The city of Delhi has many beautiful buildings and monuments.

Look at the pictures and complete the name of some famous buildings and monuments of Delhi by writing the correct letter in the box provided.

1. Qutub ☐

2. Red ☐

3. Lotus ☐

4. India ☐

5. Humayun's ☐

6. Jantar ☐

a. Tomb

b. Mantar

c. Minar

d. Temple

e. Fort

f. Gate

Whiz quiz

Find out the names of the rulers who built these buildings.

Literacy Skills

35 Closed Lists

DATA HANDLING

Closed lists have a fixed number of things such as days of the week.

Look at these closed lists and fill in the missing words.

1 Months of the Year

- ....
- ....
- ....
- April
- ....
- June
- ....
- ....
- ....
- October
- November
- ....

2 Names of Indian States starting with M

- Meghalaya
- Manipur
- ....
- ....
- ....

3 Chess Pieces

- King
- Rook
- Bishop
- ....
- ....
- ....

4 Primary Colours

- ....
- ....
- ....

5 Suits in a Pack of Cards

- Spades
- Clubs
- ....
- ....

6 Secondary Colours

- ....
- ....
- ....

Whiz fact

Pluto was once in the list of planets. Scientists decided that it was too small to be a planet. So, the closed list of nine planets is now a closed list of eight planets.

Sports

36 Olympics Special

Various sports are played at the Olympics by many countries.

Read the lines and match them with the correct pictures.

1 The mascots of the 2024 Olympic Games is Olympics Phryge, which takes the form of a Phrygian Cap, a symbol of freedom, in the colours of the French flag - blue, white and red.

2 The 2024 Olympics are held in Paris.

3 The host of the 2020 Olympics was Tokyo.

4 The Olympics were first held in Athens.

5 The Olympic flag has five rings.

a

b

c

d

e

Whiz fact

Surfing, which returned to the Olympic Games in Tokyo, was included in the Paris Olympics, and held a whopping 9750 miles away from Paris in Teahupo'o, Tahiti!

Literacy Skills

37 Space and Days

In Hindi, the days of the week are named after some planets, moons and stars.

Read the clues and write the Hindi names of the days of the week.

1 *Soma* is the Moon

2 *Mangal* is Mars

3 *Budh* is Mercury

4 *Guru* or *Brihaspati* is Jupiter

5 *Shukra* is Venus

6 *Shani* is Saturn

7 *Ravi* is the Sun

a Monday ....

b Tuesday ....

c Wednesday ....

d Thursday ....

e Friday ....

f Saturday ....

g Sunday ....

Whiz quiz

The English names for four out of seven days are named for gods in Norse mythology. Match the names of the gods with the day of the week.

1 Tyr

2 Odin or Woden

3 Thor

4 Freya or Frigga

a Wednesday

b Thursday

c Friday

d Tuesday

38 Going to America

Look at the picture clues and complete the interesting facts about America by writing the correct letter in the box provided.

	Clue	Box	Picture		Option
1	The Statue of Liberty is in this city	☐		a	Dollar
2	The capital of USA is named after this leader	☐		b	Hawaii
3	The flag of the United States	☐		c	Hollywood
4	The national anthem of America	☐		d	Stars and Stripes
5	A place known for its film industry	☐		e	George Washington
6	The currency of the USA	☐		f	New York
7	A state made of islands and volcanoes	☐		g	The Star-Spangled Banner

Whiz fact

The National Bird of USA is the bald eagle.

Life Skills

39 Being Safe

Being safe is one of the first things people learn. Babies learn to hold the hand of an adult when they are learning to walk so that they do not fall. There is always more to learn about safety because as we grow, we do more things and go to more places.

Tick (✓) the pictures that show the safer thing to do and write why it is safe.

1 a  ☐ b  ☐

2 a  ☐ b  ☐

3 a  ☐ b  ☐

4 a  ☐ b  ☐

5

a 

b 

6

a 

b 

7

a 

b 

8

a 

b 

Whiz fact

While travelling in a boat, we wear life jackets or safety vests. They are brightly-coloured and we should always wear them for our safety.

40 India Extremes

India Focus

India is the seventh largest country in the world.

Match the pair of India extreme ***opposites*** *and write their names using the words given in the help box. One has been done for you.*

1 Coldest, Dras, Ladakh, –45°C → b

2 .... Mount K2, 8,611 m above sea level

3 ...., Mawsynram and Cherrapunji

4 Northernmost point, Siachen Glacier

5 .... point, Ghuar Moti, Gujarat

6 Smallest state, Goa

a .... point Indira Point, Great Nicobar Island

b .... Phalodi, Rajasthan, –51°C

c Lowest, Kuttanad, Kerala, 3 m below sea level

d ...., state Rajasthan

e Driest, Thar Desert

f Easternmost point, Kibithu, Arunachal Pradesh

Help box

Westernmost	Largest	Highest	Hottest	Southernmost	Wettest

Whiz fact

The southernmost point of mainland India is Kanyakumari. The distance between the Siachen Glacier and Kanyakumari is 3,043 km.

41 Anagrams

An anagram is a word or phrase formed by changing the order of the letters in another word or phrase. For example, 'listen' is an anagram of 'silent'.

CRITICAL THINKING

Write one anagram using the letters of each of these words. One has been done for you.

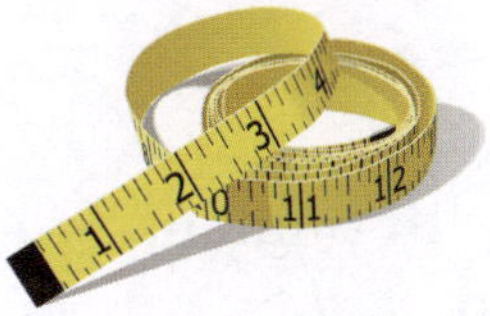

1. I N C H

   C H I N

2. V A S E

3. A R C

4. B R A G

Now, write two anagrams using the letters of each of these words.

5. O W N

6. O P T

7. F L O W

8. I N K S

9. M E A L

Whiz fact

A palindrome is a word that is the same whether you read it backwards or forwards, for example the word 'refer'.

42 Northeast India

The northeast is one of the most beautiful regions of India. It is connected to the rest of India through a narrow stretch of land in West Bengal. This region has eight states—the Seven Sisters and Sikkim.

Read the clues and fill in the blanks using the words given in the help box.

1. Arunachal Pradesh shares its border with Bhutan, China and Myanmar. The 400-year-old .... Monastery is situated here.

2. Shillong, the capital of Meghalaya, has fresh breezes, hilly roads and misty skies. It is known as the .... of the East.

3. The name Mizoram means 'land of the hill people'. Mizoram's traditional dance is called the cheraw. Dancers jump between long .... sticks.

4. Nagaland shares a boundary with Assam, Arunachal Pradesh and Myanmar. The .... Festival is celebrated in this state.

5 Manipur shares a border with Myanmar. The royal game of .... played on horseback originated in this state.

6 The Kaziranga National Park, the home of the one-horned .... is in Assam.

7 In the tiny state of Tripura, most of the people speak either Kokborok or ....

8 Sikkim lies in the lap of the majestic Himalayas. The third-highest mountain peak in the world, the .... looms over this state.

Help box

Hornbill	Kanchenjunga	Tawang	Scotland
Bengali	rhino	polo	bamboo

Whiz fact

The river Brahmaputra flows through two northeastern states of India—Assam and Arunachal Pradesh.

World Around Us

43 Sri Lanka, Here I Come!

Sri Lanka is India's neighbouring country to its south.

Fill in the blanks with the correct answers. The map and pictures will help you get some answers.

1. The flag of Sri Lanka has a .... lion/tiger.
2. The executive and judicial capital of Sri Lanka is .... Colombo/Sigiriya, while the legislative capital is Sri Jayewardenepura Kotte.
3. Sri Lanka has a .... cold/warm climate.
4. Sri Lanka .... is/is not an island country.
5. The .... Palk Strait/ Bering Strait separates India from Sri Lanka.
6. Sri Lanka is one of the largest exporter of black .... coffee/tea.
7. .... Ceylon/Bali is the old name of Sri Lanka.
8. .... Blue lotus/ Marigold is the national flower of Sri Lanka.

Whiz fact

The Sri Lankan flag is symbolic of the native people of Sri Lanka, the Sinhalese.

Skills

44 Mind and Body

SELF AWARENESS

Write the names of these yoga poses using the words given in the help box.

1 ....

2 ....

3 ....

4 ....

5 ....

6 ....

Help box

Plank | Tree pose | Bow pose | Cobra pose | Warrior pose | Cow pose

Whiz fact

Yoga has made a lot of positive impact in recent times. 21 June, the longest day of the year in the northern hemisphere, has been adopted by the United Nations as The International Day of Yoga worldwide since 2014. Also, the 2026 Asian Games to be held in Seoul will include yoga as a non-competitive sport. Who knows, yoga could well become a competitive sport in the years to come!

45 Religions Around the World

People around the world follow different religions. Some of them were started by men.

Look at these boxes and finish the lines about some religions. One has been done for you.

	What was his name?	Where was he born?	What religion did he start?	What are his followers called?
	Prince Siddhartha or Gautama Buddha	Lumbini, Nepal	Buddhism	Buddhists
	Prince Vardhamana Mahavira	Vaishali, Bihar, India	Jainism	Jains
	Jesus Christ	Bethlehem, Palestine	Christianity	Christians
Islam	Prophet Mohammad	Mecca, Saudi Arabia	Islam	Muslims
	Guru Nanak Dev	Nankana Sahib, Pakistan	Sikhism	Sikhs

1 Prince Siddhartha or Gautama Buddha was born in Lumbini, Nepal. He started Buddhism. His followers are called Buddhists.

2 Prince Vardhamana Mahavira was born in .... He started ....
His followers are called ....

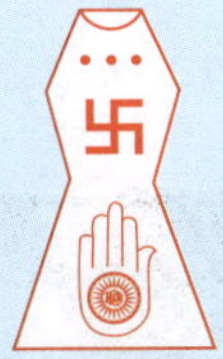

3 Jesus Christ was born in ....
He started .... His followers are called ....

4 Prophet Mohammad was born in ....
He started ....
His followers are called ....

5 Guru Nanak Dev was born in ....
He started ....
His followers are called ....

Whiz fact

Some other major religions of the world are:

Hinduism, the religion practised by more than 75% of Indians, many Nepalis, as well as others around the world;

Judaism, whose followers, called Jews, are spread all over the world;

Shintoism, practised mostly in Japan;

Taoism and Confucianism, practised in China;

Voodoo, practised mainly in Benin, Togo, Ghana and Nigeria

India Focus

46 Rabindranath Tagore

Here are some facts on the life of Rabindranath Tagore.

Put them in the correct time order to learn about this great Indian.

Rabindranath Tagore

Visva-Bharati University

1 He won the Nobel Prize in Literature in 1913 for his beautiful collection of poems called *Gitanjali*.

2 He founded the Visva-Bharati University at Santiniketan in 1921.

3 A song written by Tagore called *Jana Gana Mana* was sung in public in 1911. It later became the national anthem of India.

4 He died on 7 August, 1941 in Kolkata.

5 Rabindranath Tagore was born on 7 May, 1861 in Kolkata.

Whiz fact

Rabindranath Tagore preferred to learn without schooling, punishment and classes. He is also known as *Gurudev*, which means 'teacher'.

47 Hidden Countries

Find the names of countries hiding in these sentences. One has been done for you.

1. They are travelling in diametrically opposite directions. 
2. What do you think, can a daydream really come true? 
3. There is a famous spa in this mall. 
4. Isn't the funfair a nice place to spend the day? 
5. This bank has a branch in all the big cities. 
6. My glasses, which I left on the table, are missing. 
7. There were nine palm trees in a row. 
8. The foods we deny ourselves are usually yummy. 
9. You will have to shun Gary until he behaves better. 
10. Although entry was forbidden, Mark got us into the museum. 
11. The pipe rusted completely, so we changed it. 
12. She trusted us, and we lived up to her trust. 
13. Oh goodness, stop it, Alyson, please behave! 

Whiz quiz

Try and hide the following countries in sentences:

MALI ....

CHAD ....

TOGO ....

CUBA ....

Learning Skills

48 Sudoku

Sudoku is a Japanese number puzzle. It has three columns and three rows in which numbers from 1 to 9 are arranged randomly without being repeated.

CRITICAL THINKING

In this Sudoku puzzle, a square is empty. Therefore, we must look for the missing number, which is 7.

1	5	8
4	2	9
	3	6

Find the missing numbers to solve these Sudoko puzzles.

1

7	6	3
4		5
8	2	6

2

9	5	7
2	8	
1	3	6

3

2	6	
4	5	1
7	3	8

Whiz fact

The first ever printed Sudoku puzzle appeared in a London-based newspaper called The Times.

49 Oceans of the World

Five oceans cover more than 70 per cent of the Earth's surface.

Look at the map of the oceans of the world and fill in the blanks.

1. The .... is the largest ocean in the world. It has more than half of all the ocean water in the world.
2. The .... is the smallest and the shallowest ocean in the world.
3. The ocean that surrounds Antarctica is called the ....Ocean. It got its name in the year 2000.
4. The .... Ocean was the first ocean to be circumnavigated by a ship and an aeroplane.
5. The .... Ocean is bounded by Africa on the west, Asia on the north and Australia on the east. It is the warmest ocean in the world.

Whiz fact

The Southern Ocean is also called the Antarctic Ocean or the Austral Ocean. Antarctic means the opposite of Arctic and Austral means south.

Quiz Yourself 1

Choose the correct answer from the given options.

1 Which northeastern state shares land borders with Bhutan, China and Myanmar?

(a) Assam (b) Arunachal Pradesh
(c) Meghalaya (d) Nagaland

2 Mickey, Stuart, Remy and Jerry are all names of which animal?

(a) Dogs (b) Cats (c) Mice (d) Horses

3 What did John Logie Baird invent?

(a) Telephone (b) Telegraph (c) Radio (d) Television

4 Which of these sea creatures has eight limbs?

(a) Whale (b) Octopus (c) Sea Horse (a) Shark

5 Which is the smallest state in India?

(a) Sikkim (b) Kerala (c) Goa (d) Tripura

6 Which is the largest ocean in the world?

(a) Pacific Ocean (b) Atlantic Ocean
(c) Indian Ocean (d) Arctic Ocean

7 What colour is the new ₹2,000 banknote?

(a) Bright Yellow (b) Stone Grey (c) Lavender (d) Magenta

8 Which city is the capital of Australia?

(a) Sydney (b) Canberra (c) Brisbane (d) Perth

9 Which Indian won the Nobel Prize in Literature?

(a) C V Raman (b) Rabindranath Tagore
(c) Kailash Satyarthi (d) Mother Teresa

10 What is the southernmost point of mainland India?

(a) Kanyakumari (b) Indira Point
(c) Cape Horn (d) Somnath

Quiz Yourself 2

Choose the correct answer from the given options.

1 For playing which sport is Saina Nehwal famous?
(a) Tennis (b) Squash (c) Badminton (d) Billiards

2 Which freedom fighter was known as 'The Iron Man of India'?
(a) Sardar Vallabhbhai Patel (b) Mahatma Gandhi
(c) Pandit Nehru (d) Lokmanya Tilak

3 What name is given to the sound made by hyenas?
(a) Roar (b) Laugh (c) Howl (d) Bark

4 Which little boy could fly, but never grew up?
(a) Tom Thumb (b) Oliver Twist (c) Mowgli (d) Peter Pan

5 Which freedom fighter and poet was known as the Nightingale of India?
(a) Bhikaji Cama (b) Sarojini Naidu
(c) Annie Besant (d) Kasturba Gandhi

6 Which state is the largest in India?
(a) Maharashtra (b) Madhya Pradesh
(c) Rajasthan (d) Uttar Pradesh

7 Which country's flag is made up of two triangles?
(a) Nepal (b) Bhutan (c) Sri Lanka (d) Bangladesh

8 Who is likely to receive a Major Dhyan Chand Khel Ratna award?
(a) A scientist (b) A doctor
(c) An actor (d) A sportsperson

9 Which is the smallest planet, named after a Roman God of the same name?
(a) Jupiter (b) Mars (c) Mercury (d) Venus

10 In which country were paper, clocks and the compass invented?
(a) India (b) China (c) Japan (d) Greece

Quiz Yourself 3

Choose the correct answer from the given options.

1 Which of these board games uses currency notes?

(a) Scrabble (b) Monopoly
(c) Ludo (d) Snakes & Ladders

2 The Palk Strait separates which country from India?

(a) Maldives (b) Mauritius (c) Sri Lanka (d) Indonesia

3 What name is given to the bony case in which our brain and sense organs are enclosed?

(a) Skull (b) Rib Cage (c) Spine (d) Knee Cap

4 In which country was Lacrosse first played?

(a) Russia (b) Sweden (c) Norway (d) Canada

5 Which feeedom fighter was the first Prime Minister of India?

(a) Sardar Patel (b) Pandit Nehru
(c) Dr Rajendra Prasad (d) Lal Bahadur Shastri

6 In the famous children's book *Black Beauty*, what type of animal is 'Black Beauty'?

(a) Lion (b) Tiger (c) Horse (d) Elephant

7 Of what material is the Taj Mahal built?

(a) Black Granite (b) White Marble
(c) Red Sandstone (d) Green Marble

8 Who was known as the 'Missile Man of India'?

(a) Dr APJ Abdul Kalam (b) Giani Zail Singh
(c) Dr CV Raman (d) Dr Hargobind Khorana

9 What is the principal food of the Giant Panda?

(a) Sugarcane (b) Potatoes (c) Bamboo (d) Maize

10 Which city is the capital of Meghalaya?

(a) Guwahati (b) Shillong (c) Itanagar (d) Aizawl

Quiz Yourself 4

Choose the correct answer from the given options.

1 Which river flows by the side of the Taj Mahal?
(a) Ganga (b) Godavari (c) Brahmaputra (d) Yamuna

2 For playing which sport is Rameshbabu Praggnanandhaa famous?
(a) Carrom (b) Badminton (c) Chess (d) Billiards

3 Which planet is known as *Shani* in India'
(a) Saturn (b) Uranus (c) Neptune (d) Jupiter

4 Of which country is Ottawa the capital?
(a) USA (b) Mexico (c) Canada (d) Iceland

5 Which of these is issued by the Income Tax Department?
(a) Driving License (b) Voter ID Card
(c) Passport (d) PAN Card

6 Which country's national anthem is 'The Star Spangled Banner'?
(a) United Kingdom (b) USA
(c) Australia (d) New Zealand

7 What was invented independently by Alexander Graham Bell and Antonio Meucci?
(a) Radio (b) Television
(c) Telephone (d) Gramophone

8 In which state is the Kaziranga National Park situated?
(a) Nagaland (b) Mizoram (c) Assam (d) Manipur

9 On which Indian bank note will you find an image of the Sanchi Stupa?
(a) ₹100 (b) ₹200 (c) ₹500 (d) ₹2000

10 Which of these sports is not considered as part of athletics?
(a) Running (b) Walking
(c) Jumping (d) Horse-riding

Answer Key

Page 9: 1. two; 2. too; 3. there; 4. their; 5. it's; 6. Its

Page 10-11: F1. MANGO; F2. WATER MELON; F3. BANANA; F4. CHERRY; F5: PAPAYA; V1. CABBAGE; V2. SPINACH; V3. POTATO; V4. PUMPKIN; V5. GINGER

Page 12-13: Answers will vary

Page 14-15: 1. chatter; 2. click; 3. trumpet; 4. crow; 5. honk; 6. bark; 7. laugh; 8. sing; 9. squeak; 10. croak

Page 16-17: 1. bones; 2. heart; 3. brain; 4. skin; 5. spine; 6. stomach; 7. lungs

Page 18: 1.v; 2.iv; 3.i; 4.ii; 5.iii;

Page 19: 1. H; 2. C; 3. O; 4. O; 5. H; 6. C; 7. O; 8. O

Page 20: 1. Monopoly; 2. Lego; 3. Scrabble; 4. Ludo; 5. Jenga; 6. Carrom; 7. Chess; 8. Snakes and Ladders

Page 21: 1. *Goosebumps*; 2. *Casper*; 3. *Hotel Transylvania*; 4. *The Witches*; 5. *Maleficent*

Page 22-23: 1. frangipani; 2. drumstick flower; 3. gulmohar flower; 4. daffodil; 5. pansy; 6. clove flower; 7. bougainvillea; 8. hibiscus

Page 24-25: 1. *The Jungle Book*; 2. *Alice's Adventures in Wonderland*; 3. *Gulliver's Travels*; 4. *Stuart Little*; 5. *Winnie-the-Pooh*; 6. *Charlotte's Web*; 7. *Peter Pan*; 8. *Pippi Longstocking*; 9. *A Bear Called Paddington*; 10. *Black Beauty*

Page 26-27: 1. Missile; 2. medicine; 3. ballet; 4. gold; 5. Nightingale; 6. Children's Day; 7. Teachers'; 8. melody

Page 28-29: 1. octopus; 2. whale; 3. starfish; 4. jellyfish; 5. seahorse; 6. shark; 7. oyster; 8. crab

Page 30-31:

B	F	Z	N	Y	T	C	W	X	U	K	D	W
O	B	A	S	K	E	T	B	A	L	L	N	G
W	G	N	Q	W	N	V	I	Q	N	I	E	X
L	H	O	U	A	N	O	L	I	N	G	O	V
I	U	R	A	T	I	A	L	H	U	L	A	O
N	K	K	S	E	S	F	I	O	A	Y	M	L
G	W	E	H	M	G	C	A	C	Z	E	R	L
G	T	L	L	S	O	U	R	K	B	Y	R	E
O	B	L	N	K	W	Y	D	E	I	Y	U	Y
L	Q	I	L	A	C	K	S	Y	O	S	G	B
F	I	N	W	I	N	D	S	U	R	F	B	A
N	N	G	K	N	Y	M	P	H	E	T	Y	L
P	O	L	O	G	A	R	I	S	O	N	E	L

1. polo; 2. rugby; 3. bowling; 4. squash; 5. billiards; 6. basketball; 7. hockey; 8. golf; 9. tennis; 10. volleyball

Page 32-33: 1. 0, 2; 2. 1, 45; 3. 2, 10; 4. 3, 10; 5. 11, 25; 6. 1, 20; 7. 1, 25

Page 34-35: 1. ✓; 2. ×; 3. ✓; 4. ✓; 5. ×; 6. ✓; 7. ×; 8. ✓; 9. ×; 10. ✓; 11. ×; 12. ✓; 13. ✓; 14. ×; 15. ✓; 16. ×; 17. ×; 18. ✓

Page 36: 1. mausoleum; 2. Yamuna; 3. marble; 4. dome; 5. minarets; 6. gardens

Page 37: 1. save file; 2. cut; 3. copy; 4. paste; 5. undo; 6. redo; 7. print; 8. close file

Page 38-39: 1. f; 2. c; 3. b; 4. e; 5. a; 6. d

Page 40-41: 1. a. penguin, it cannot fly; 2. a. shark, it cannot live on land at all; 3. b. monkey, it has hair on its body;

4. b. dolphin, it breathes with lungs;
5. d. spider, it has eight legs;
6. d. jellyfish, its body is not covered with a shell

Page 42-43: 1. Tennis; 2. Wrestling; 3. Badminton; 4. Cricket; 5. Shooting; 6. Chess; 7. Golf; 8. Boxing

Page 44-45: 1. 
Russia
; 2. 
Italy
;
3. 
Bangladesh
; 4. 
Turkey
; 5. 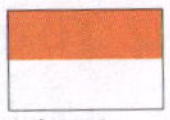
Indonesia

Page 46-47: 2. raincoat; 3. armchair; 4. inkpot; 5. wheelbarrow; 6. necklace; 7. buckle; 8. wallet; 9. sandwich; 10. toast

Page 48: 1. north; 2. east; 3. west; 4. centre; 5. south

Page 49: 2. d, Hampi with Chariot; 3. b, Sanchi Stupa; 4. a, Magalyaan; 5. e, Rani Ki Vav; 6. f, Red Fort

Page 50-51: 1. ouch!; 2. ta-da!; 3. eek!; 4. boo-hoo!; 5. yahoo!; 6. oh no!; 7. wow!; 8. shh!

Page 52-53: 1. Mercury; 2. Venus; 3. Earth; 4. Mars; 5. Jupiter; 6. Saturn; 7. Uranus; 8. Neptune

Page 54-55: 1. b; 2. a; 3. e; 4. c; 5. d

Page 56-57: Across: 4. javelin throw; 5. relay; 6. hammer throw; 7. marathon; 8. long jump; 9. shot put

Down: 1. discus throw; 2. hurdles; 3. pole vault

Page 58: 1. Driving licence; 2. Passport; 3. Voter ID; 4. PAN Card

Page 59: 1. cow, Moscow; 2. Canada, can; 3. Brazil, Ra; Brasilia; 4. wash, Washington D.C.; 5. China, chin; 6. err, Canberra

Page 60-61: Across: 1. green dot; 6. ingredients; 8. feedback

Down: 2. nutritional value; 3. brand name; 4. best before; 5. MRP; 7. net weight

Page 62: 1. d; 2. a; 3. b; 4. e 5. c

Page 63: 1. c; 2. e; 3. d; 4. f; 5. a; 6. b

Page 64: 1. January, February, March, May, July, August, September, December; 2. Maharashtra, Madhya Pradesh, Mizoram; 3. Pawns, Queen, Knight; 4. red, yellow, blue; 5. Diamonds, Hearts; 6. violet, orange, green

Page 65: 1. b; 2. e; 3. a; 4. c; 5. d

Page 66: 1. *Somwaar*; 2. *Mangalwaar*; 3. *Budhwaar*; 4. *Guruwaar*; 5. *Shukrawaar*; 6. *Shaniwaar*; 7. *Raviwaar*

Page 67: 1. f; 2. e; 3. d; 4. g; 5. c; 6. a; 7. b

Page 68-69: 1. b, walking on footpath;
2. a, not keeping hands out of a vehicle;
3. b, crossing road at a zebra crossing;
4. a, wearing a helmet while riding scooter;
5. b, wearing a seatbelt;
6. b, walking in the same direction as others;
7. a, not listening to loud music on a bus;
8. b, cleaning hands before eating food

Page 70: 1. b, hottest; 2. c, highest; 3. e, wettest; 4. a, southernmost; 5. f, westernmost; 6. d, largest

Page 71: 2. save; 3. car; 4. grab; 5. now, won; 6. top, pot; 7. wolf; fowl; 8. sink, skin; 9. male, lame

Page 72-73: 1. Tawang; 2. Scotland; 3. bamboo; 4. Hornbill; 5. polo; 6. rhino; 7. Bengali; 8. Kanchenjunga

Page 74: 1. lion; 2. Colombo; 3. warm; 4. is; 5. Palk Strait; 6. tea; 7. Ceylon; 8. Blue Lotus

Page 75: 1. tree pose; 2. warrior pose; 3. plank pose; 4. cobra pose; 5. cow pose; 6. bow pose

Page 76-77: 2. Vaishali, Bihar, India, Jainism, Jains; 3. Bethlehem, Palestine, Christianity, Christians; 4. Mecca, Saudi Arabia, Islam, Muslims; 5. Nankana Sahib, Pakistan, Sikhism, Sikhs

Page 78: 1. c; 2. d; 3. b; 4. e; 5. a

Page 79: 2. **Canada**, What do you think, can

a daydream really come true?; 3. **Spain**, There is a famous spa in this mall.; 4. **Iran**, Isn't the funfair a nice place to spend the day?; 5. **China**, This bank has a branch in all the big cities.; 6. **Chile**, My glasses, which I left on the table, are missing.; 7. **Nepal**, There were nine palm trees in a row.; 8. **Sweden**, The foods we deny ourselves are usually yummy.; 9. **Hungary**, You will have to shun Gary until he behaves better.; 10. **Denmark**, Although entry was forbidden, Mark got us into the museum.; 11. **Peru**, The pipe rusted completely, so we changed it.; 12. **USA**, She trusted us, and we lived up to her trust.; 13. **Italy**, Oh goodness, stop it, Alyson, please behave!

Page 80: 1. 1; 2. 4; 3. 9

Page 81: 1. Pacific Ocean; 2. Arctic Ocean; 3. Southern Ocean; 4. Atlantic; 5. Indian

Page 82: Quiz Yourself 1:

1. b; 2. c; 3. d; 4. b; 5. c; 6. a; 7. d; 8. b; 9. b; 10. a

Page 83: Quiz Yourself 2:

1. c; 2. a; 3. b; 4. d; 5. b; 6. c; 7. a; 8. d; 9. c; 10. b

Page 84: Quiz Yorself 3:

1.b; 2. c; 3. a; 4. d; 5. b; 6. c; 7. b; 8. a; 9. c; 10. b

Page 85: Quiz Yourself 4:

1.d; 2. c; 3. a; 4. c; 5. d; 6. b; 7. c; 8. c; 9. b; 10. b